MEAN STREETS

A Collection of Poems
from the Heart

By Charles Garbutt Young,
a.k.a. Randy C. McNeil

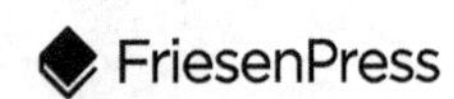

One Printers Way
Altona, MB R0G 0B0
Canada

www.friesenpress.com

First Edition — 2022

ISBN
978-1-03-911722-8 (Hardcover)
978-1-03-911721-1 (Paperback)
978-1-03-911723-5 (eBook)

1. POETRY, CANADIAN

Distributed to the trade by The Ingram Book Company

TABLE OF CONTENTS

//

INTRODUCTION

This book is dedicated in loving memory to twenty-two street friends who were taken long before their time was due.

Four were murdered.

Six committed suicide.

Six overdosed.

Six died in drug- and alcohol-related accidents.

In their premature demise, this world lost some very special people.

We miss you all

1970–2000

Mary. A Linda. G Tab. O
Neil. A Brett. H Conrad. P
Cam. B Brian. M Lorry. P
Jimmy. B Jeff. M E. Rodstrum
Louie. B Lonny. M Danny. S
Tom. B Jimmy. O Virginia. S
Melody. C Rob. O Gordan. W
Steven. K

I would also like to dedicate this book to the survivors of our early days growing up in East Vancouver. British Columbia, Canada, a.k.a the Renfrew Parkers, the 22nd and Rupert boys (the 22 Gang), and the Norquay Parkers.

When I look back on those days and the wild lifestyles we were all living, it is truly a miracle that we were not all in a grave.

These are some of my favorite lyrics and poems. Some are about war and love while others are about real life situations. Still others carry a message of freedom. These poems are not categorized. They are mixed up so that readers will not get stuck in any one particular message I am trying to convey. I hope you enjoy this short work. If you are affected in a positive way by it, then it has all been worthwhile. For these are truly a collection of *poems from the heart.*

BUTCH

From one who knew his waddled walk,
his crooked grin as he smiled or talked.
Those droopy shoulders,
those half-slit eyes,
that face
that smile
that laughter
and then,
oh God,
I wish butch was back with us again.

In fond and loving memory of
Gorden Kenneth Wood (Butch)

RANDY'S GOT A GUN

A pistol in your hand, thoughts go through the head.
What would life be like when this death we have shed?
Will the flames consume us? It really don't seem fair, but at this point I'm uptight, so little do I care.

Chorus:
What's it all about? There's no place left to run.
Look out, I'm pissed off.
Randy's got a gun.
It's all that noise and confusion.
It's crowding out my brain. It's the high nights and the low days that are driving me insane.

It's the tough talk
The cool walk
I'm really trying to refrain.
It's the new styles on the old frame.
I'm tired of all the games.

What's it all about? There's no place left to run.
Look out, I'm pissed off.
Randy's got a gun.
It's all that noise and confusion.
It's crowding out my brain. It's the high nights and the low days that are driving me insane.
It's the right girl on the wrong night.
There's no place for love in a street fight.
It's the cheap booze and expensive cocaine
that turns your dreams into a life of jokes.

It's the good friends, oh, who will do you harm.
And the woman you love in someone else's arms.

What's it all about? There's no place left to run.
Look out, I'm pissed off.
Randy's got a gun.
It's all that noise and confusion.
It's crowding out my brain. It's the high nights and the low days that are driving me insane.

It's the men in blue, yelling, "Face down!"
on a one-way street in Chinatown.
With the rain falling
on your face
while the record plays amazing grace.
As the shots ring out in the dead of night,
your frightened soul takes an uncertain flight.

What's it all about? There's no place left to run.
Look out, I'm pissed off.
Randy's got a gun.
It's all that noise and confusion.
It's crowding out my brain. It's the high nights and the low days that are driving me insane.

As the shots ring out in the dead of night, your frightened soul makes an uncertain flight.

So, what's it all about? There's no place left to run.
Look out, I'm pissed off.
Randy's got a gun.

LIVING IN THE PAST
(LOOKING FORWARD TO THE GRAVE)

Here I sit, and it looks like I've come to the end of the road.
My mind is in a rear-view mirror that won't leave me alone,
Lorry, you're the only thing I've got going for me in this life.
Can we start over again without the pain and strife?

I need your love so badly;
you're the only thing I crave.
I've got one foot in the past
and the other in the grave.

The river Styx is looking pretty good tonight.
I know, baby, that you and I feel right.
Moonbeams sparkle across the gentle flow.
If you turn your back on us, girl, how can our love grow?

I need your love so badly;
you're the only thing I crave.
I've got one foot in the past
and the other in the grave.

Reflecting on the pain that's deep within my heart,
my vision of the future, girl, is that we'd never part,
I refuse to live without you; life just wouldn't be right.
A carbon-monoxide cocktail to get me to the night.

'Cause I need your love so badly;
you're the only thing I crave.
I've got one foot in the past
and the other in the grave.

YOU NEVER PLANNED TO DIE

Didn't you see the red light?
Because you went and drove ahead.
If you were paying more attention, ***Butch,***
you wouldn't now be dead.
Tell me, was it one too many beers?
Is that the reason why?
Because we know the night you hit the wall,
you never planned to die.

Neil, couldn't you see it coming?
There was a hooker by your side.
One time you had the girls for free, and
now you're paying for the ride.
Some ***China White*** to help your flight;
you were flying pretty high.
That's why we know the night
you juiced the white
you never planned to die.

Danny was eating reds like candy
and chugging Christmas cheer.
It's party time for six more days;
we'll drink into the new year.
So high you couldn't roll over,
they said that's the reason why
you drowned in your own vomit, Dan,
but you never planned to die.

My merry, precious ***Mary,***
wasn't one man good enough?
He said that he would kill you;
did you have to call his bluff.
You had one too many lovers,
so he stabbed you in your side.
Well, we know the day,
your man found out
that you never planned to die.

STREET UNIVERSITY

All the homes are broken; strife is in the air.
The children bond together, a brotherhood to share.
The culture of the gun, a needle and despair.
Hope is full of contradictions, so little do they care.

The street is like a potion,
that's numbing their emotion.
While looking for promotion,
they slip into misery.
Can't they see?
They graduated from "Street University."

The rage that consumes him comes from deep inside.
Only at the sight of blood can his lust be satisfied.
Morals, truth, and mercy are replaced with gutter pride.
The streets demand your soul; they will not be denied.

By now he should be crying.
Inside he knows he's dying.
When did he stop trying?
That's the mystery.
Can't he see?
He graduated from "Street University."

History comes around,
and our streets are the battleground.
The casualties of war
are the friends that are no more.

It's not with the navy's ships or planes.
The stench of death remains the same.
Look at me; I'm crying.
Inside I know I'm dying.

The street is like a potion that's killing my emotions.
While looking for promotion,
I slipped into misery.
Can't you see?
I graduated from "Street University."

STREETS

The rain, it falls to wash you,
but still you won't come clean.
I've lived your games, obeyed your rules, and for that I feel obscene.

Loitering on your corners,
rebellious and proud.
There is too much anger on you streets;
the boys are getting loud.

Squealing all four tires
in that fast, stolen car.
Robbing your neighbour's treasures
on dreams of going far.

The little girls are hustling.
Yes, they're trying to act older.
Little boys dressed all greasy
with egos growing bolder.

Fighting on your streets, I'll never be the same.
First you start with fists and boots,
then end with knives and chains.
You haven't always been like this,
but then, what could be worse,
smashing up the pizza joint
or stealing some lady's purse?

Ripping off just-built houses,
for their brand-new shiny rugs.
Phone the fence, cop a stash, and
spend three days on drugs.

It's a never-ending circle that happens everywhere,
and only those affected are the ones who seem to care.

To see all sides, the good and bad,
to survive gross defeats,
yes, me and the boys were one tough bunch,
but then, we grew up on the streets.

PICTURES

A picture is worth a thousand words,
at least that's what they say.
I'm looking through the pictures
of my friends that passed away.
Each frame tells a story,
but the story can't be heard
unless the memories of those we knew
are somehow put to words.

With every picture comes a story,
a memory of how things used to be.
But what will they see
when they look at pictures of me?

When I see those smiling faces,
peering back at me
and the moment that's etched in time,
for our posterity,
the camera cannot tell us
of their pain that's deep inside,
how they lived, their hopes and dreams,
or how tragically they died.

With every picture there's a story
of what these faces used to be.
But what will they see
when they look at pictures of me?

We keep a catalogue of prints
from the cradle to the grave.
The snapshots of a life
are little portions that we've saved.
Some say that they are gone from us,
but that's not true at all.
There are portraits staring back at me
from the mantle by the hall.

Every picture tells a story
of how things used to be.
But what will they see
when they look at pictures of me?

ANGER

My soul is free, yet I am bound in chains.
I bend with the wind; I drown in the rain.
Days of torrential sunlight are revealing all my shame.
I'm embarrassed by the lack of love inside my golden gilded cage.
Once my anger was confined, but now my anger is enraged.

Please speak so very softly, or don't speak to me at all.
I'm so tightly undone that my back is against the wall
I'm feeling egotistical and yet feeling very small.
I can't compete with reason; you can be insane at any age.
My anger used to be confined, but now my anger is enraged.

Confusion and despair fits me like a leather glove. I cried into the lonely night and kissed the stars above. I wished upon your purest dreams the cold realities of love.
This depth of pain that I am feeling is impossible to gauge.
My anger used to be confined, but now my anger is enraged.

Your love is as unforgiving as the waves upon the sea.
The caressing of the beach is done in two-part harmony.
You cast away my love from you, thinking you'll be free.
Desiring to turn a leaf and start with a clean page.
My anger was confined, but now my anger is engaged.

MY TURN TO DIE

The passage way we all must enter,
the ancients called death's door.
Man has learned to prolong life but cannot stop death.
Death's for sure!

We carefully lay out our plotted lives, thinking all is fine.
Never weighing out our eternal end,
until death says, "***You're mine.***"

It matters not how great our life was, rich in wealth and friends. We'd give it all for one more day; we don't want life to end.

But the inevitable is crystal clear, even though we asked the question "Why?" A voice echoes from behind death's door: "It's your turn to die!"

August 7, 1998

O'CONNOR SONG

The three pillars of O'Connor
lie broken, their spirits fled.
Was it the thunder of Tiranis,
from my heart to the head?

Or the Formorians of the North Sea,
lords of darkness and death?
Were you taken by force
or at your own bequest?

Was it the strong winds of the Sidhe?
Did they bear thee up to take?
Where dips the rocky highlands
of sleuth wood by the lake?

Where the wandering water gushes,
from the hills above Glen-car
and your voice with faery laughter,
on the wind doth travel far?

Ye were as strong as Cuchulainn and as brave as Fionn.
As wild as Boadicea,
now never more do ye roam.

Like an eagle without feathers
and a trout without fins,
were your roots so near the surface
that you could not let someone in?

You had blessed ones who loved you,
like the rain clouds they cried.
Your memory: gold in their rainbows,
as dear as the grass, the mountainside.

Do you yearn for the living,
or do you battle all night?
And the great halls of Valhalla,
or is there absence of light?

Are thy robes bathed in sunshine,
or does thy soul writhe in pain?
If you could do it all over
would you choose death again?

Sons of the emerald island,
our love for you still strong.
Never sail off our heart's horizon;
live ye forever in O'Connor's song.

The following poem is dedicated in fond memory of a family who lost three sons over a period of three years due to self -inflicted gunshot wounds to the head.

Tranis Was the Celtic god of thunder. Thus, the first stanza of the poem explains symbolically their demise through a wound like lightning to the head.

The Fomorii are the Celtic gods of darkness and death (verses five and six). They lived in the extreme north and killed the sailors whose ships sailed off the edge of the world.

Sidhe are the equivalent of fairies whose strong winds were needed to steal away newborn babies.

Verses 11 to 14 and verses 1, 2, 28, and 29 are from the poem "The stolen child" by William Butler Yeats.

Cuchulainn is a Celtic battle hero who possessed superhuman strength.

Fionn was a Celtic battle hero who lived from AD 224–283 and was the grandfather of Cuchulainn.

Boadicea was the Celtic warrior queen who united the Celtic clans of England into a general uprising against the Romans.

Valhalla is the place where dead warriors abide, eating, drinking, and fighting against each other until the final battle of humankind against the gods that destroys the world.

LEST WE FORGET BRETT

The phone it rang, and J. R. said
you wouldn't be coming by no more.
I'd never hear your voice again
or find you smiling at my door.

The truth of it all was painfully clear:
you left the living to embrace the dead.

They told me you didn't want a funeral but that something should be said.
Your brother bore your ashes nigh;
I poured you in your mother's hands.
She broke him and wept over wasted years
that only a mother could understand.

The Renfrew Parkers were all there,
although a few of them were missing.
They hadn't learned yet to unlock the doors
of their self-imposing prisons.

They stood in line to receive a turn
at spreading your ashes all around.
Each face was lined with tear stains
as you were sprinkled on the ground.
We spread you at the smoke tree,
(you know) that old, familiar haunt
where in days gone by
we'd laugh and get high and take in tomorrow's light.

They gathered themselves around me,
and I asked them all the same:
How could such a thing happen?
Or was their comradeship a game?
Was there no one he could turn to?
Was he afraid that all would laugh?
Call him weak,
abuse his feelings
as though they were discarded trash?

No sooner had I finished the words,
when your wake had thus begun.
They glorified the wasted years, though
they just buried another mother's son.

I'm so sorry I wasn't there for you.
It's the one thing I will always regret.
So, I wrote a few lines
to remember those times,
lest we forget Brett.

RENFREW

Why should I worry? Why should I care?
This life I'm leading is still going nowhere.

This girl said she loved me,
but once again I am alone.
She needed multiple lovers,
And now she doesn't even phone.

The rain that is falling
can't wash away the stain.
Have a heart torn wide open,
nor the easing of the pain.

But there's a place I can go
where the gang calls home.
It's down to the park, a place of our own.
Things are less complicated;
the little creek ripples by.
There's a forest in the gully,
where we'd sit and get high.

Of the sixty solid friends I had,
spread out through several circles,
twenty-two were cut down hard;
the rest of us are miracles.
Sniffing gas and airplane glue
until our minds were blank.
The drugs that we ingested,
the liquor that we drank.

We went down, dog and dirty,
even when the odds were stacked.
But we never lost the turf fight,
a friend was always at our back.

If it was more than one on one,
your belt or blade was fine.
A picket fence or broken glass
could buy a little time.

We knew each other's secrets
and the pain that's deep inside.
We respected one another
and matured our boyish pride.

They would give you their last dollar,
last toke, or can of beer.
Hell, we even shared a woman
that we mutually held dear.

But people move in all directions
and disappear on the horizon.
Old loyalties are shattered,
ties broken beyond repair.

I'm looking through the memories
of those days of wine and glory.
Some are dressed in prison greens;
some we buried with their story.

Some tried to break the cycle
and move their kids away.
Others moved in to fill the gaps;
the cycle's here to stay.

We weren't alive in that life.
Some saw death as their only end.
How I loved them all like brothers.
They were what I call *true* friends.

IN LOVE WITH GHOSTS

You arise from the abyss
of fading memories,
haunting corridors,
refusing exile, banishment.

I feel your breath on the morning breeze.
Words beckoning me are indiscernible.
You are dead; intangible.
You are alive; forever young.
Gazing into your ageless faces,
I feel those kindred spirits.

A choir of distant laughter
entwined in foregone times
transcends and illuminates
youthful mirth and merriment.
And once again we are together!
Yes, once again together!
And once again I feel the pain.
Once again I feel the pain.

Transmissible forms from dimensions of obscurity
like moist mist, rising, from the shadowy water cold.
You fear you'll be forgotten, dissipate into nothing.
I'm afraid to let you go.
Which part of me is you?
Through the void in my heart, the voyage back convicts me.
A prisoner of my conclusion, I'm still in love with ghosts.

For all my fallen friends, February 18, 1998.

THE DEAD

The dead are always with me.
I think about them all the time.
What do they feel in death's embrace?
Can they feel at all?

I see their faces, hear their voices.
Memories, they move through my soul.
Deeds we did together, laughter, stories untold.

Like a miser hoards his gold,
I have secreted you away
in he deepest chambers of my soul,
where with me you will stay.

The dead are always with me.
I think about them all the time.
Your flesh consumed, your bones lie cold
beneath this hollow ground.

Time moves forward, and I grow older,
but you remain the same.
Alive in that place of perpetual youth
where the shadow of age is ashamed.

Like a flower, rare, you blossomed
under the timeless sky.
A fragrance, so daring and wild.
My love for you keeps me alive.

For the dead are always with me,
I think about them all the time.
We sit in the parlor of my heart and
relive the days gone by.

We toast and consume the nectar of the gods
and divide the spoils of war.
We frolic in the pools of the canyon
where your voices are heard once more.

And yet each time we visit, I'm that much closer to the day
when the flame of my life will fade from my eyes.
Then with you I will stay.

IF YOU COULD SEE
(THROUGH HIS EYES)

He stands in the shadows and moves about through time.
He walks through your valleys;
your mountains he has climbed.

The heavens reveal his secrets;
the earth trembles at his name.
Mankind is prostrate before him,
and every creature is ashamed.

He sees through our rebellion;
there is a firc in his word
that devours those before him,
who took no heed to what they heard.

If you could see through his eyes,
what would you see?
The wholesale slaughter of humanity.
No place to hide for you or for me
above the clouds or beneath the sea.

So, tell me, where did love go?
So, tell me, why did hate grow?
Together you and I must always be!
Together bound in love for eternity.

Everybody has a vision
of how they want their life to be.
The past is sealed behind us,
yet the future is ours to see.

The prophet reads the road map
to all our hopes and dreams.
Well-laid plans of mice and men
are cruel and petty schemes.

We want the choice of freedom,
but it will not set us free.
You must stand in the docket
to be judged for eternity.

If you could see through his eyes,
what would you see?
Through misty eyes I see
the destruction of humanity.
No place to hide for you and me
above the clouds or beneath the sea.

So, tell me, where did that love go?
So, tell me, how did hate grow?
Together you and I must always be!
Together found in love for eternity.

THE THINKER

A very flexible man came up to me.
And this is what he had to say.
The good die young.
The bad die old.
But then either way, hell knocks on the grave!
For no one is perfect; we'll all have to pay.
Or is it the other way?
Then, contemplating what he said,
he bid me a fair day.
And, stepping into a thinker's trot,
he thought himself away!

REBIRTH

My mind was torn, filthy rags, but
Jesus made a tapestry.
My heart was frozen stony ground, but
Jesus grew a garden.
My soul was lost in darkness, but
Jesus gave it light.
My life was dead in trespasses and sin, but
Jesus arrayed it in his righteousness.
Hatred ruled my very being,
but with the love of Jesus,
"I am broken."

SPIRITUAL QUEST

On the path of coloured leaves,
dying moss, and naked trees,
it's the season birds fly south,
the season when twigs fall.
I listened very carefully, but I could not hear you call.

I searched the cloud-clapped mountains;
I combed the valleys below.
I tried to listen for you
through the silence of the snow.
Body numb and heart cold,
my soul was feeling small.
I turned an ear toward heaven, but I still couldn't hear you call.

The streams are overflowing;
the valleys are plush with green.
The birds are busy among the treetops,
but for me they can't be seen.
It's a season of new life
that God gave to one and all.
I know that I would have new life,
if only I could hear you call.

ALL I KNOW

All I know is that I love him
because he died for me.
All I know is that he shed his blood that day on Calvary.
All I know is that he sacrificed,
so all the world could live.
Yes, what a prize to pay for love; that's what my Jesus did.
I know that they scorched him
before they hung him on a tree.
All I know is that a crown of thorns,
he wore to set me free.
All I know is that he paid the price,
my sins he would forgive.
Yes, what a price to pay for love; that's what my Jesus did.
All I know is that I love him;
he was nailed instead of me.
And that he died upon a rugged cross
for all the world to see.
He sacrificed himself, so that through him I might live.
Yes, what a price to pay for love, but that's what my Jesus did.

VISIONS OF A NO-MAN

On a tiny little island
in the ocean of the sky,
there lived a king of all men.
Such a king, he couldn't lie.

Now this king he had a vision
upon his throne of golden fleece
of love, an understanding,
and of universal peace.

But he was troubled by a galaxy
not near or far
and of the twinkle in the middle,
a bright and wondrous star.

Knowing beneath the beauty,
the evil that lurked with him,
so wicked was this evil,
that the king, he named it "sin."

Now troubled for their problem,
he sent a message loud and strong.
But the people wouldn't listen,
for to them there was no wrong.
They were masters of all masters
ever since their time began.
But the king of all men was saddened,
for he knew they were but men.

"Visions of a no-man!" the king cried out in distant rage.
"Angels are the winged ships that fly with me this day.
The wicked of the foolish world, don't want me, so it seems.
So, into battle I must fly to destroy their wicked dreams."

The wicked of the planet
fought back with heart's desire
until the king made an open pit
and cast them into its fire.
And those who loved the
king and gladly let him in,
why, he took them all to heaven
and away from death and sin.

"Visions of a no-man!" the king cried out in distant rage.
"Angels are the winged ships that fly with me this day.
The wicked of the foolish world, don't want me, so it seems.
So, into battle I must fly to destroy their wicked dreams."

THE RACE

Masters of organized confusion.
Dreams of owning one's own mind.
About his fear in the ocean of the sky washed up on the beach of time.

Their coats were many colours,
but within they were all the same.
The strong strove against one another,
and weaklings played their games.

The power was dissipated down to four
armies battling for time and space
When the armies of the world reach the Middle East,
why, this will end the race.

ARMAGEDDON

To be a bird, unshaven wings.
The eagle span is wide.

The bear that stalks
the Middle Eastern valley
is deceived by Marxist pride.

The Bible tells the truth, you see; John
didn't lie in Revelation.

Together with the
kings of the east, it's a worldwide devastation.

So, there's not too much that
we can do except our sins to mend.
To live in love our remaining years.
Soon all our fears will end.

ETERNITY

Time, from the past to the president, is the same.
It follows our lives and knows all that we've done.
Eternity is its name, and eternity is forever.

Our lives submit to the hands of time, which quickly pass by,
for we are but a vapour here, born and then we die.
But eternity lives forever.

All the life we mortals waste, as broken dreams fade by.
The poor must starve to feed the rich,
to fulfill the last four eyes.
But eternity sees forever.

What can matter change a piece, and love,
Well, we can't even live together.
Can we love our fellow man?
The verdict read said, "Never."
Therefore, punished for eternity,
and eternity lasts forever.

PREJUDICE

The little girl lay crying;
the old man dried her tears.
He sat her on his one good leg and asked her of her fears.

"The children, they don't like me;
they always call me names.
And with me they won't share their toys or let me play their games.
They tease me about my colour,
but I know we're all the same within."

The old man bowed his lined gray face.
"Ah," he whispered. "Sin."

Now if being prejudiced was confined to one area,
then all the world would know
that it's but an evil hatred
from the one who rules below.

It's because it lives in every land that people cannot see
the way it defiles the tenderest heart and makes their spirits flee.
So do not blame the children,
for they do not understand
that by the hatred in the home,
it thrives to spread across the land.
"My little girl, you have a friend,"
he said, "who lives in heaven above.
He'll never leave you or forsake you'
he cleans your soul with love."

The little girl, she thanked him
and went contentedly on her way.
Yes, she had found a friend in Jesus
to help along life's way.

She never saw the old man again,
but that didn't make her feel alone.
For in her heart she knew who he was
And that he'd be back to take her home.

SO

So easy to lust.
So easy to lie.
So easy to cheat.
It's too hard to die!

So hard to forgive.
So hard to be true.
So hard to stay strong.
It's so hard to be you!

So easy to steal.
So easy to sin.
So easy to run.
We're destroyed from within.

LONELINESS

There is a fear that dwells within
us all that most of us do hide.
A fear that creeps within the heart
and keeps our spirit inside.

A fear that births the demons
of jealousy, hate, and greed
and grows a thornbush in our
hearts that spreads its evil seed.

While in the days of darkness,
isolation fans the flame.
And in the hours of confusion,
loneliness calls your name.

Sweet freedom or sad sorrow,
oh, those memories of pain.
You built your life on emptiness,
and lost all you thought to gain.

Please believe in him, just someone,
for he dwells too much in shame
Sweet Lord, he needs your freedom,
for loneliness called his name.

PLACE SETTINGS

Serve up my enemies on
plates of gold and silver.
All through my life, they fought me hard, but
with their death I'll have the plunder.

Feelings raped and misused, manhood disrobed.
Spirit deranged through lusty living memories implode.

Serve up my love on plates of diamond with black pearl.
I loved all those whom I called a friend,
even if it never showed.
Love adorned, then tossed aside,
betrayal held so dear. That elusive golden love,
the banishment of fear.

Serve up my feelings on plates of friendship and remorse.
We walked the path of darkness,
from the truth my soul did hide.
So, I built my castles tall and barred the gates from deep inside.

We all have felt that hatred, we sometimes feel for one another.
Like the coldness of the snow, when all that is green gets smothered.

Serve up my life on plates of bone with blood and flesh.
I serve not him who gave me life, my soul's in such a mess.
No values left to stand on; life is wasted every day.
In every bend along the road, yet another friend has slipped away.

Serve up my soul on the platter of eternity.
How great God's throne to sit above the glittering, jeweled sea.
Thus, God himself prepared a place for the sons of liberty.
A place where there is peace, love, and tranquility without carnality.
For if we are bound up in our flesh,
how can our souls be free?

THE PRIZE

I am who I am,
and there is no denying it.
But my spirit and my flesh, they fight each other.
So, what's the use in tryin'?

My mind appears to be strong,
my body fit and well.
But my mind is the key to eternity,
be it heaven or hell.

So, why am I the battleground,
so small within my mass?
The key is that I have a soul that will forever last.

Evil tries to break us,
to make our hearts do wrong.
I know within my jaded past, I've added to this song.

But fear not, O twisted soul,
with your heart pressed against the wall.
Place your faith in Jesus;
he is the mightiest of all.

THE OTHER ONE

If your eyes are used
for sight, then see.
If your lungs are used for
breath, then breathe.

If your legs can go
the distance, walk with me.
If your back cannot carry the
weight, then give me your load.

If your arms hold mistrust,
I'll wrap you in compassion.
If your heart is filled with pain,
we shall laugh away your tears.

If your mind is all confused,
I will share my understanding.
If your life has passed you by,
I will lie with you in your grave.

PEOPLE

People live and
people die.
People love and
people cry.
People walk and
people fly.
People are clever;
people are sly.
People are aggressive;
people are shy.
People tell the truth;
people often lie.
People understand;
people can't see eye to eye.
People starve;
people loosen their belt and tie.
People hate people.
People pray to the sky.
Have you people ever stopped to ponder,
why?
People, why?

FIELDS OF GREEN

He laid in flowed fields of green
staring at the moonlit sky.
Why did I ever leave my love
for such a lonely place to die?

Then he dreamed of the one
true love that he had,
dreamed of the love he could hold.
Then he touched on several younger loves
and likely stories untold.

But for a second,
did your memory leave his side
as he stared into the moonlit sky.
Oh, sweet Jesus, comfort me,
for soldiers do not cry.

Then he dreamed of your face,
your beauty, your grace.
He longed for your lips, ruby red.
Oh, sweet Jesus, just to kiss her
once more before the Red Cross
tags me as dead.

I just have to have her.
I don't want to die.
But there he lay
in flowered fields of green
staring at the moonlit sky.

When I awoke in the morning,
I went straight for Mom's room.
There was something that I had to say.
But when I reached her doorway,
I could hear my momma pray.

Oh, sweet Jesus,
I just got this letter.
Why'd he have to die?
Oh, sweet Jesus, comfort me,
for a soldier's wife don't cry.

It's strange when you're six years old,
not knowing what's wrong or right.
That's why I never told my momma
the dream of Dad I had that night.

I'LL BE THERE

I stood gazing upward, eyes forever on high,
Till stardust descending gave light to blinded eyes.

I stood gazing down
at the darkness below,
on the abyss of forever on death's overflow.

I stood in the midst of the flaming sky.
Men burned with boils, the ground cracked and dry.

The smoke and the ash blocked out the light
so that even at midday, it appeared to be night.

Then I stood in the middle of the wide-open spaces,
the bombed-out dreams with the skeleton faces,
and hope, once melted, had again solidified
in the words of a warlord,
so more children would die.

Then I stood in the face of the raging sea as
she gave up her dead and declared victory.

O death, where is thy sting?
O grave, where is thy victory?
Forever are you vanquished, and the human soul set free.

Then I rode in the midst of the gleaming white horses and witnessed the king
destroy all Satan's forces.
I was there in the thick of the valley of slaughter
to watch the bloodletting
of Babylon's daughters.
The fowls were summoned, the great feast was set,
the vultures descending, the city beset
by two hundred million,
the demonically suicidal,
their carnage lay deep,
to the horse's bridle.

The small and the great men, the bound and the free,
merged their puddles of flesh into one bloody sea.

Thus, I saw in the vision God's finger of power, the dragon cast down,
his city destroyed in one hour.
The great king triumphant, the heavens proclaimed,
with the heavenly choir,
praising God in Jesus's name.

BILLY'S SONG

There's a hole in Daddy's arm,
where all the money goes.
Jesus Christ died for nothing
(some suppose).

Little pictures have big ears,
to turn back the wasted years.
Blue songs, route songs, are playing on Dad's radio.

The little boy lay crying,
"What's my daddy doing in jail?"
Sunday school told Billy, but his Jesus never fails.

So, why is dad so far away? Our house just ain't at home.
Me and sis, without a dad, and Mom's left all alone.

There is a hole in Daddy's arm,
where all the money goes.
Jesus Christ died for nothing
(some suppose).

Little pictures have big ears, to turn back the wasted years.
Blue songs, rude songs, are playing on Dad's radio.
Come Sunday morning,
Billy asked the church to pray.
"I'd like us all to pray for my dad, though he is miles and miles away.
Pray the Lord would strengthen him
and move him to a farm,
'cause sitting in those dirty cells,
will only do more harm."

A preacher man came calling
to the work farm on that day.
All the men they gathered in to
hear what he would say.
He preached about the love of God, his sacrifice
for sin.
The Lord was there to meet their
needs if only they'd let him in.

There's a hole in Daddy's arm,
where all the money goes.
Jesus Christ died for nothing (some suppose).

Little pictures have big ears, to turn back the wasted years.
Blue songs, rude songs, are playing on Dad's radio.

Everybody knows the truth
about what happened on that day.
Some men laughed, some men scarfed, and some men walked away.

But there was one man
near the front repenting of his sins.
Veinless arms stretched to
the sky as the spirit entered in.

Praise the Lord forever, Billy's dad will never be the same.
He got baptized in a watery grave and came up in Jesus's name.

The transformation was so great,
they released him from the farm.
Praise the Lord forever,
Jesus healed up Daddy's arms.

There was a hole in Daddy's arm,
where all the money used to go.
Jesus Christ didn't die for nothing,
don't you know?

Yes, little sister has big ears;
Jesus turned back the wasted years.
New songs, good songs, are now
playing on Dad's radio

ONE-WAY TICKET TO THE SUN

While waiting for the sun to rise,
I fell into a dream.
I woke up in the land of death
beside a blood-filled stream.
The land was overrun with flames
that flickered all around.
And when I looked inside myself,
my soul was chained and bound.

Well, thanks for the one-way ticket to the sun.
After death I thought there was
no life, but mine has just begun.
Be ever so careful of the things you say and do,
for although you may
escape them in life, in death all will come back to you.

The vision was so real
that I thought I felt the pain.
The flames consumed my flesh,
but then my flesh appeared again.

The fire licked my flesh once more from off my boney frame.
The cycle will forever continue,
and I am the one to blame.

Well, thanks for the one-way ticket to the sun.
After death I thought there was
no life, but mine has just begun.
Be ever so careful of the things you say and do,
for although you may
escape them in life, in death all will come back to you.

The moral of the story is plain
for those who wish to see,
that our journey upon this earth is but a test for eternity.

There is a better way of living
that truly makes you free.
It's free for the taking if free is what you really want to be.

TREE PEOPLE

There once was a tree
the nun should see.
As it sat on a mountain,
as high as it could be,
the sun would shine,
the winds would blow.
The snows they fell,
to melt and go.
Yet no matter how hard it tried,
the little tree couldn't grow.
Now as he strained to grow, he surely had to know
that no one can grow without love.
So, grow,
and love a tree.

REVOLUTION'S – REVELATION'S

Renew, revolutions.
Rebuild, rethink, re-educate, revolutionaries.
Realign, recapture, reinvent, revolutions.
Regroup, revamp, restructure, revolutions.
Reorganize recharted, reckless, revolutions.
Retire, rape, rifle raising, revolutionaries.
Reject, ridiculous random retaliation.
Remove revengeful resolve.
Remain real.
Read, redefine revolutions.
Rcalize realistic revolutions.
Rearm, redeploy, righteous revolutions.
Release reinvigorated revolutionaries.
Revolutions, revelations, remedies, reluctant Revisionists.

THE FOOL

I saw your face in poignant beauty
stretched across the evening sky.
I heard your voice and gentle laughter as the day breeze passed me by.
The forest and the meadows all smell as sweet as you,
and I wish you were with me.
I dreamed of things that we could do.
A walk up on the mountain,
going bareback for a ride.
Sitting around an open fire
with you by my side.

Flashes in the night time of the things we say and do.
Yes, I walked the mountains
and the valleys, dear, but all I saw was you.

When the heavens open up to me,
the stars all look the same.
The wind, it rustles through the pines
and gently calls your name.

The clouds, they all remind me
of your skin as pure as snow,
but I change just like the seasons, dear;
that is why you had to go.

Remind me of your sweet love,
Which burns the passion of my mind.
For no other love I have met
who is so beautiful and kind.

He showed me how a man can be a fool, and
this I've grown to know.
For I have been a foolish man,
my love, for I'm the fool who let you go.

?

The wind whispers to me
of destiny, of things to come that I must be.

But all I see is you!

The sun shines brightly, beckoning me to grow.
But no one in the world can grow without love.

This I've grown to know!

The rain, it falls to give us life from thunder clouds above.
And yet I ask myself again and again . . .

What is life without your love?

VIETNAM

Although I am eighteen,
I am still not a man.
Can't drink publicly
Till I'm twenty-one.
But when all hell breaks loose,
they will ship me away.
Goof boots,
duffel bag, and gun!

SLEEPLESS

Dawn has finally broken.
The rain tumbles gently down
into the loving arms
of an ever-thirsting ground.

Birds chirp in the distance
and drink the morning dew.
As the little wisps of wind dust off
the lanes and avenues.

The flower-scented air, to
the senses, fresh and clean.
People are stirring in their houses,
but for me they can't be seen.

The aromas from the kitchen
excite my palate. They waft by
as the colours of the rainbow
illuminate the morning sky.

Robins peck a crust of bread,
a kind soul tossed upon the lawn.
Not having slept a wink all night,
I meet them with a yawn.

Walking rain-washed streets,
listening to the cobblestones speak,
but they can't tell half the story
of the rolling deck in all its glory.

Seaweed on a sea breeze,
lodges in my throat.
Wool cap about my head and ears,
I button down my coat.

There is not a single tavern open.
I already had one too many a nip
with my face toward the open sea,
I head home to my ship.

THE MIGHTY HUNTER

One day while I was moving
down an ever-thinning trail,
a little to my left I spied
a fluffy little tail.

On further investigation,
as I drew so ever near
the tail was the other end
of a healthy baby deer.

As it got a little closer,
I could plainly see
the little guy had caught his hoof
inside a rotten tree.

Approaching him very slowly,
I gently set him free.

And as he turned to run away,
I quickly shot him dead.
"It's a cruel, cruel world,
little fellow. A cruel, cruel, world," I said.

THE LAW

He rode into town
wearing a star.
By the look of his clothes,
this man had ridden far.

He climbed off his horse
and into the street, and
with each step he took, the dust rolled off his feet.

All eyes were upon him, and this he knew.
Over the post his reins he threw.

He was a middle-aged man, tall and lean.
Hands old and tattered, face lined and mean.

He looked down at me with a cold killer stare
while removing his hat from his long silver hair.
"I'm looking for a man who calls himself big Jed."

Across the street in the saloon,
"Stranger, I said."

He reached the doorway, looking frail and thin.
Adjusting his guns, he proudly walked in.

Two shots were fired, and not a second or more,
wounded and bleeding, he walked back through that door.

"My job in this town is finished," he said.
"The man that I sought now lies there dead. On his tombstone I want it to say,
'Killed by his father.'"
Then he sadly rode away.

LIVE BY THE SWORD!

His face was lined and windblown, cold fall coffee, can of beans.
He sold his gun for gold and silver; he sold his gun for dreams.

To die in a blaze of glory, to a faster gun well known,
to become the fastest gun alive, for this he left his home.

Killing for him became easy, but it wasn't always that way.
He used to farm a tract of land before the bank took it away.

He wandered many sleepless nights, and in order to survive,
sold his gun and haunted men; that's how he stayed alive.

Somewhere along the dusty trail, the truth in him got lost.
His hatred conquered all he was; he didn't count the cost.

A transformation had taken place; a killer had been made.
A conscience seared, a heart of stone to help him play his trade.

One day upon the dusty street, he faced two guns alone.
His palms were wet and sweaty; his thoughts referred him home.

He never heard the deadly shots; he never felt the bullets' pain.
. He never even cleared the leather, but he could feel his life force drain.

If only he could warn them, those men who gunned him down, that one day they would be lying with their faces in the ground.

THE TIME IS PAST

He sits alone in the empty house,
the TV for a friend.
The family is all gone out;
the day is almost at an end.

He has so much to offer,
but his offers can't be heard.
By the hearts he loves the most dearly,
so there is a silence around his words.

He's the lonely man
with a smile on his face.
Such a lonely man,
he's so out of place.
His time has come;
his days are few.

Will his words have any meaning when his lonely life is through?

There's discipline in his words;
there's a deep wisdom for his age.
But it was never written down
like some ancient Grecian sage.

Or an Elizabethan playwright who wrote,
"All the world's a stage."

Desiring to share with a loved one
what was gathered over the years,
he sits alone in the empty house
and fights back silent tears.

He's a lonely man
with a smile on his face.
Such a lonely man;
he is so out of place.
His time has come;
his days are few.

Will his words hold any weight
when his lonely life is through?

The shade of death merges
with the silhouette on the wall.
Within the black and the shadow,
you cannot see his right arm fall.

A long black box, a marble stone,
and in the earth, he was tucked away.
Some say we buried an old man,
but we buried wisdom that day.

He was the lonely man
with a smile on his face.
Such a lonely man,
he was so out of place.
His time has come; his days are few.

Will his words hold any meaning
when his lonely life is through?

YOUTH IS GONE

Youth is gone! It was frivolously spent
on riotous living,
and now it's old and bent.

We admire youth's luster
like some distant star
and recall our youth from memories afar.

Our children are born,
and we watch them grow.
while trying to shield them
from youth's awful blow.

Spring forth in the dawn,
youth dances through the day.
and in twilight's last gleaming,
youth flickers away.

Youth is but a vapor;
it's here and then it's gone.
Like the shadow of the night
between the dusk and dawn.

One long look backwards
to ponder youth's event.
Youth loved and squandered,
youth wasted and spent.

LOOKING BACK

Just a casual backward glance
that caught a distant memory
of people, things, and places,
of how life used to be.

I find I'm walking backwards
a little more each day.
My back toward the future,
my eyes longing for yesterday.

Ghosts dance on the horizon;
I used to know their names.
The sun sank into darkness
as they danced in twilight's flames.

What is it about the past
that captivates the soul?
It's the memories of the past
that make the future whole.

Never forget the past;
it made you who you are.
People spun through your life
and wished upon your star.

You're a composite of people
who caused each other pain.
Sometimes there was sunshine,
but mostly it was rain.

Woven into each other's life,
you're knitted to their soul.
So, keep alive those memories;
it's what makes the future whole.

SORRY

Sorry for the things I've done
and all the things I've said.
Sorry for the silly games
and messing with your head.

Sorry for the many times
I filled your heart with fear.
Sorry for the many times
I should have held you near.

Sorry for the many times
I knew the truth but lied.
Sorry for the many times,
because of me you cried.

Sorry for the many times
I never listened with my heart.
Sorry for my doubts and
him tearing our love apart.

Sorry in our vocabulary
has become something absurd.
It placate those we've hurt
with the soothing of a word.

Sorry heals up nothing
if not delivered with the deed.
Sorry helps to break the ground,
so love can plant a seed.

But *sorry*, which is often said,
will only last so long.
Sorry can't be a martyr's cross
or a reputation's song.

Now I can tell you honestly
this is not just another story.
from the bottom of my heart,
my love,
I'm telling you,
I'm *sorry.*

WHO AM I?

I'm at the birth of every man.
I intrude on all his dreams.
I see all his hopes and follies.
I see everything between.

I bring men to the darkness,
and because of me, they fear.
I'm the shadow hanging over.
I stalk man all his years.

I harvest his murders.
I harvest his plagues.
The famines and the wars.
Man's filling of the graves.

I have slain men by the billions,
yet I want this race to thrive.
For it's the death of every human
that is keeping me alive.

I CAN SEE

All live under the same sky,
with canyons deep
and mountains high.
The valley floor,
the forested woods,
the meadow green
with flowered hood.

The rivers, lakes,
and mountain streams,
all clear as glass
in some light sheens
as phantom icebergs,
through waters ply
those ghostly clouds,
from ocean high.

Till fiery sphere,
doth melt below
horizon's line,
as streamers glow.
Handy withdrawals
at night's advance
be freckled heaven's,
shine and dance.

The bullfrogs croak,
And the cricket's song
doth tell us all
that naught is wrong.
The feathered fowl
and furry beast,
do lay their heads
where danger's least.

And thus I sat
in raptured awe
in marveled deep
at what I saw.
And pondered why
with human eye
we fail to see
as time goes by
that what is here
will soon be gone.

The buttercup,
the blue jay's song,
the leviathans that swim the seas,
nature grand
in greed doth flee.

And man,
noblest of
all creatures,
great and small,
he rapes the land
of all he sees,
pollutes the air
with his factories.

He wages war
on fellow man
to gain the bounty
from their land.
Perplexed to know
the reasons why
all live under the same sky.

WAR

WAR: *That chivalrous act of noble savagery.*

The indispensable dispenser
of cruelty and barbarism.
Of cowardliness and bravery.
Of honor and dishonor.

WAR: *The ultimate human contest.*

For the metal of mankind
is measured by man's willingness
to subjugate his fellow man.
To kill or face being killed.

WAR: *The madness, a mindless folly of man.*

The earth opens her mouth impartially,
devouring the flesh of the fallen.
The rivers of fresh human blood.
A nectar for the demons of the abyss.

Bleached bones huddle together
under a canopy of blackened skies
and burnt vegetation.

Dreams, one so pure and noble,
are set adrift on a notion of death.
Sailing on hollow winds and vile breezes.

The rain, once looked favourably upon,
now descends from the heavens.
The killing fields are now a quagmire of death, mud, and blood.

WAR: *Plagues the very existence of mankind.*

His war machines
and his weapons of mass destruction
now hold within themselves
the ability to annihilate their creators.

Mars, infamous god of war,
the earth is drunk with the lives
of those who have fallen
upon your unholy sword.

War admits its cruelty
and romantic savagery.
There is no hypocrisy in war.
War is devoted to the annihilation
of the human race and spirit.

And well man points an accusing finger
at the many reasons for war.
War whispers an enduring truth:
"I exist for one reason only . . ."

It has always been in the heart of a man
to freely kill his brother.

TIME

The future, tomorrow,
becomes the present: today.

The history of the past
is sealed forever
in the twenty-four hours
of yesterday.

BIOGRAPHY

My chest hurts.
My chest hurts.
I can no longer run.

But terror struck my body
when that policeman
pulled his gun.

I don't want to steal,
but my habit's getting strong.
I'm only fifteen,
and all the things I've done wrong.

Someday I'd like to be famous
and even write a book.
But I guess it'll never happen
if I don't stop being a crook.

LOVE WALKER

She was a one-time beauty.
She was a one-time queen.
She was the foxiest lady
your eyes had ever seen.
She's living on a mountain;
her life didn't have a care.
Her feet started slipping,
and now she's sliding nowhere.

Yeah, *she's a nowhere woman*
in a nowhere land.
She's going nowhere fast,
and she don't understand.
She's on a loser's highway;
she can never win.
She hangs her loving on the
outside, but she's dying within.

Now she's a pill-popping come on
with the glazed green eyes.
She wears her fashions like skin
and hikes her skirts for the guys.
She doesn't know who she's with
and tries to forget where she's been.
She's got to sear that conscience, bang her up until she wins.

She's a nowhere woman
in a nowhere land.
She's going nowhere fast,
and she don't understand.
That it's a loser's highway.
She can never win.
She hangs her loving on the outside
while she's dying within.

They say she's now on the hustle,
for a man from uptown.
She tried to make him her own,
but he's made her his clown.
She gives her body to the street
for the love of this man.
And while she dreams about his touch,
she takes it any way she can.

She's a nowhere woman
in a nowhere land.
She's going nowhere fast,
and she don't understand.
She's on a loser's highway.
She can never win.
She hangs her loving on the outside,
but she's died within.

LADY

My soft and lovely lady,
come and life with me in fields
that are newly born green,
and we will taste each other's love like we have never seen.

Lady,
my soft and lovely lady,
why did you have to leave?
You didn't have to go.
You could have stayed beside me.
Don't you know I love you so?

Lady,
I'll catch up with you, baby.
When I do you'll tell me
why you went away
and all those foolish reasons,
of why you couldn't stay.

Old lady,
my soft and lovely lady,
come and lie with me in fields
of newly born green.
We will taste each other's love
like we have never seen.

Lady,
my sentimental baby,
your letter said you love me,
and this I know is true.
Oh heavens, my sweet lady,
I just want to be with you.

Oh, lady,
my soft and lovely lady.
now that I've got you back,
I'll never let you go.
I'll place you on a pedestal
because I love you so.

Oh, lady,
my soft and lovely lady,
commonly with me in fields
of newly born green,
we will taste each other's love
like we have never seen.

UNKNOWN WARRIOR

I have risen above the earth,
which I was made of.
I have bloomed like a flower
in the setting sun.
I have shed my pre-dawn myths,
and I have walked naked
till all my quests are done.

I am life; I am love.
I am the earth, the sea, and the sky.
Now you tell me I must die.

The day will come when all life dies, the day that death is born. Then I'll find the answers, so you say. While dreams never come true, only premonitions do. And the smell of a dream gone bad has burnt the nostrils of my mind.

Mother, you're kind to give me birth but never life.
Teachers gave me facts but never wisdom.
Eyes gave me sight but never helped me to see.
I know in my heart is a stone, and I know my soul's not free.

Yet I am life, and I am love,
I am the earth, the sea, and the sky.
I am master of creation,
But now you tell me I must die.

The day will come when all life dies, the day that death is born. Then I'll have the answers, so you say. While dreams never come true, only premonitions do, periods and the smell of a dream gone bad have burnt the nostrils of my mind.

Now I'm slowly slipping
to where the sun never shines.
I can hear it in the morning;
they'll all read about me in the headlines.

My soul, groping at freedom,
is now stripped away from me,
falling prey to the unknown paths of eternity.

Eternal darkness covers my inflamed and tortured mind.
Unknown warrior for all time, please be kind.

STRIDER

No creature was his equal;
they all feared his name.
Life was all that they had left,
all the power he would gain.
The fierceness of this warrior,
the land of the midnight rider.
All those who opposed this man
would feel the steel of strider.

Oh strider, oh strider,
warrior from the land
of the midnight riders.
Oh strider, oh strider,
the ring you seek, and oh so well,
can only be destroyed in a molten hell.

Evil in the hand of sorrows
where the blackest shadow grew.
This warrior had the power,
this the demon knew.
Through the haunted night,
the soulless shadows flew.
Seek out the prince and take his life
is what they had to do

He climbed the cliff and loosed the ring,
courage he never lacked.
Without a moment to lose,
the shadows pressed the attack.
The earth began to tremble,
black shadows taken down.
As for the warrior strider, he could not be found.

Oh strider, oh strider.
warrior from the land
of the midnight riders.
Oh strider, oh strider,
the ring you destroyed, and oh so well,
has doomed you to die in a fiery hell.
Why, strider?

LIVING IN WASTED TIME

The dragon slowly slumbers,
into a deep blood-filled grave.
Triumphant warrior upon its back, so bloody and so brave.
Climbing from the evil beast
to admire his greatest kill,
his soul cried out for ages past,
no longer to be still.

He who drinks the dragon's blood
would have immortal fame.
Mixed I saw with dragons blood
all power shall you gain.
Little known is the price he'll pay
for this latest crime.
Forever dawns hell on earth
and living on wasted time.

Dipping hands into the blood,
he clenched his dusty throat.
Pain tore every muscle;
his form began to bloat.
Years turned into great horns,
his flesh into green scales.
Feet and hands grew great claws
as hard as iron nails.

Now he knows the price he'll pay,
for this latest crime.
Forever dawns his hell on earth
and living in a waste of time.

No one was there to help him,
this his soul did know.
He failed the test of chivalry,
and now darkness ran the show.
Thoughts for lost in power,
scarce gone through the mind.
Unrighteousness was found in him,
And his godly soul went blind.

Little known is the price we'll pay
for our list of crimes.
Failing to learn from days gone by
and living in wasted time.

RETRIBUTION DAY

Well, it's the verbal diarrhea
that you feed to us each day.
We really love our country,
but we see it going your way.
You're the voice of the people,
but the people have no say.
We let you in to help our lives,
and now you plan to stay.

Well, retribution day's the day
your petty power crashes down.
Retribution day's the day
it all lies prostrate on the ground.
Retribution day's the day
when all deceptions will end.
Retribution day's the day,
no more fences we can mend.

I saw a people who had
lost sense of direction.
Last seen was the rejection,
from a husband for his wife.
We live in a world that is seething with infection.
There is no more moral interjection
in this toilet bowl called life.

(Yes) Retribution day's the day
your petty power crashes down.
Retribution day's the day
it all lies prostrate on the ground.
Retribution day's the day
when all deceptions end.
Retribution day's the day
no more fences we can mend.

Your addiction to contradiction,
while you tell us to relax.
Do you ever tire of bogus facts,
or covering up your tracks.
The day is fast approaching,
retributions the solution.
New world order step aside, for an apocalyptic revolution.

retribution days, the day,
your petty power crumbles down.
Retribution days, the day,
when you lay prostrate on the ground.
Retribution days, the day,
when your deceptions at an end.
Retribution days, the day,
when all our fences he will mend.

DECISIONS

I saw a man making bridges out of matchsticks.
Every time we tried to cross, a spark would burn it down.
This old man is sifting through the blackened ashes
to spread them on his fallow ground, to help his garden grow.

I saw a girl who had slept with her first lover.
It's the paper cuts in life that seemed to hurt the most.
I saw a woman who couldn't shake her marriage demons.
She'd escape them in the evenings
with her papercutting ghost.

Isn't it funny how people's broken dreams
can make your dreams come true?
And the pain we suffer early in life
is there to polish through. In a world where our decisions,
his between right and wrong,
and the trials of this vale of tears
are what helps to make us strong.

I saw a little boy who wouldn't share with other children.
He died alone in his twilight years, not having any friends.
I saw this man's possessions that he toiled all his life for.
The people who were next in line removed them with the trash.

I saw a man who shared all he had with people.
He died alone in his twilight years,
outliving all his friends.
I saw this man's possessions, not just things but loving people.
The people who were next in line
forgot his memories of love.

Isn't it funny how people's broken dreams,
can make your dreams come true
and how life is often measured,
by the things we say and do
in a world where our decisions
are hinged between right and wrong,
and the trials of this vale of tears
are what help to make us strong?

SHE THRILLS ME

Her kisses are as soft as velvet.
Her touch penetrates my soul.
In her eyes I see true love.
She's the half that makes me whole.

She's my lady, and I love her, period. She doesn't have those lover fears.
She's my lady, and I love her. She still thrills me after all these years.
Oh yeah, she still thrills me after all these years.

In her hair, harvests of grey.
She's too mature to wash away.
The wedding vows we keep
keep the loving where we sleep.
Her dress size is always changing,
but I thank God, she stays the same.

She's my lady, and I love her, period. She doesn't have those lover fears.
She's my lady, and I love her. She still thrills me after all these years.
Oh yeah, she still thrills me after all these years.

COWBOY QUEEN

I was her first true love;
she was my teenage queen.
She was my goddess of the night;
I was the devil in her dreams.
She was heading for the top
in long hair and faded jeans.
She was going to live her life,
so she became a cowboy queen.

She had the looks and the style.
She could sing it by the mile.
She had the beauty and the grace,
but someone put her in her place.
She had to serve us up the man;
you think by now she'd understand.
She had to go ahead and
take him all the way
just to get a honkytonk
where she could play.

My dreams can break your heart.
They can make you whole or tear your soul apart.
He doesn't care about her life.
She's just a side dish from his wife
as she becomes yet another notch
on his womanizing knife.

She had the looks and the style.
She could sing it by the mile.
She had the beauty and the grace,
but someone put her in her place.
She had to serve us up the man;
you think by now she'd understand.
She had to go ahead and
take him all the way
just to get a honkytonk
where she could play.

So, how's life on the ranch?
We know you're not there by chance.
Now, I'm not one to crush a dream,
and life is never what it seems,
but you and I both know
you settled for something in between.

'Cause you had the looks and the style.
You could sing it by the mile.
You had the beauty and the grace.
Oh, you should have slapped his face,
He's the lowest kind of man.
You'd think by now you'd understand.
That no one has the right
to take your dreams away.
And you had the gift
to take your songs and play.

BACKSIDE OF THE GHETTO

It's 8:30 in the morning, and I'm already high.
Standing on the corner, the smell of yesterday passes by.
Chico was in the alley, playing with his blade,
waiting for his girls to trick, so he could get paid.

The shops are starting to open on this grubby little street.
They'll be glad to take your money before you go down in defeat.

It's 11:30 in the morning, and
I'm really coming down.
I've been waiting for the runner
who scores his stuff uptown.

There is a commotion in the alley, so I look around the bend.
There is Chico, knifing Reggie, and I thought the two were friends.

Chico points in my direction,
and says, "Yo, now you be cool."
I say, "Hey, Chico, I saw nothing. You know I ain't no DA's fool.

It's the backside of the ghetto,
the baddest part of town.
Some people try to break free,
so they lay their bodies down.
If the drugs don't kill you,
the men in blue are in your face,
They're always after information,
but they don't live here in this place.
A guy could always start a stable
or run numbers on the side.
But the competition is entrenched,
and in the ghetto, you can't hide.

This dude tried to be a player,
and he got more than just the beats.
For him the way out of the ghetto,
was by dying on its streets.

Run, runner, where is the runner?
Now I've got the shakes.
A couple of scores and I'm out of here
no matter what it takes.

A little white to call me down,
I mellowed out my place.
I laid my lady, jacked the tunes,
and tripped out of the race.

It's the backside of the ghetto,
the baddest part of town.
Some people try to break free,
so they lay their bodies down.
If the drugs don't kill you,
the men in blue are in your face.
They're always after information,
but they don't live here in this place.
A guy could always start a stable
or run the numbers on the side.
But the competition is entrenched,
and in the ghetto, you can't hide.

POCKET NUKES

Come on, baby;
the future's here.
Stop living in the past.
Try a couple of pocket nukes,
and give your head a blast.

Pocket nukes:
the high of the future. Pocket nukes,
here to stay.
Pocket nukes,
I can't resist them.
I like to get nuked every day.

Nuke sheets,
they are red on one side and green on the other.
A couple of hits, and your mind nuked your mother.
Writing in sliding, through
the slipstream of space.
You're an atom,
you're a neutron, oh, I misplaced your face.
Starlight descending, reality bending.
The colours all fade into black.
I'm repeating my name and address,
hoping to find my way back.

Reality check coming down to Ground Zero.
I'm not the greatest hero.
Nor the highest priest to Nero.
I wasn't in space, but I did find her face.
I picked it from the collage of life
amid all the pain and strife.
You sit out from them all,
and you told me you'd call.
But the phone's been disconnected
since you tore it from the wall.

Nuke sheets,
they are red on one side and green on the other.
A couple of hits, and your mind nuked your mother.
Writing in sliding, through
the slipstream of space.
You're an atom,
you're a neutron, oh, I misplaced your face.
Starlight descending, reality bending.
The colours all fade into black.
I'm repeating my name and address,
hoping to find my way back.

The bells were always charming,
and the voices in her mind
kept her in the void of space.
She also lost the time
looking at the sacred shrine
the statue of her face.
She never came back to reality;
a spirit had taken her place.

Now she's riding and sliding
through the slipstream of space.
She's an atom;
she's a neutron'
she misplaced her face.
Her starlight is descending;
her reality is bending.
The colours all faded to black.
She's repeating her name
and her address,
never to find her way back.

WEEKEND WARRIORS
{SIDEWALK COMMANDOS}

We own these streets in avenues.
Call him on our turf.
He paid the dues.
Can somebody face down,
to us that's news.
Paper says this is a bad hood.
To us that's a great review.
People are free to walk in the daylight.
Sidewalk commandos own the streets at night.
Weekend warriors,
Looking for a street fight.
On these streets down is up, and wrong is right.

If you don't know where you're going,
the road you're on will take you there.
Violence, pain, and misery
is all they've learned to share!
A one-way street full of heartache and despair.
They murdered their own conscience;
it's no wonder they don't care.

There was a house close to the firehall.
A junior Rambo,
with guns on every wall.
"Help yourselves, boys.
Spread the plague around.
With a trunk full of weapons,
the road only leads down.
So, you've got yourself a Colt .45
Does that demand respect?
Point it in my direction,
and I'll break your scrawny neck.
You can't shoot straight anyway,
you drugged-out mess.
You're using too much product,
Look at him confess!

If you don't know where you're going,

the road you're on will take you there.
Violence, pain, and misery
is all they've learned to share!
A one-way street full of heartache and despair.
They murdered their own conscience;
it's no wonder they don't care.

So, you went and broke the street code.
Did you forget where you was at?
My lifelong friend,
your life must end.
This ain't no lovers' spat.
You punked-out bad,
you bitching queen,
you dirty stinking rat.
The .45, you thought so cool
will surely lay you flat.

If you don't know where you're going,
the road you're on will take you there.
Violence, pain, and misery
is all they've learned to share!
A one-way street full of heartache and despair.
They murdered their own conscience;
it's no wonder they don't care.

NUCLEAR

I've prayed for those who toiled
and fought on foreign soil.
For those who were sent to
battle in others' lands.
For those who
washed with bloodstained hands.
The hardships
that have faced you.
Your memories of pain.
Total death and
damned destruction
But we'll do it all again!
It seemed a waste
to spend your lives on
such misery and sorrow.

To crush the dreams
of a broken man,
for he fought for
a better tomorrow.
And for our
new tomorrows.
Can your souls
now lay at rest?
For the dogs of war are hungry
in spite of all your best.

Our new sophisticated
weapons, those billion-dollar
pillars of death.
With our ability
to extinguish all life,
after this, what's next?

SHE ROCKS ON

She was poised in the doorway,
like some magazine queen.
She was the hottest little number;
she was into the scene.
Her lips were ruby red;
her dress was also tight.
She could be your Miss Innocent
or rocky through the night.

***She rocks on, rocks on. Just a few more hours till the breaking of the dawn.
She rocks on, rocks on. When the morning sun awakens you,
you'll arise to find her gone.
She's rocked on.***

She could rock you like a demon,
but she had an angel's face.
She had to get laid every evening,
even if that someone took my place.
She had jade-green eyes,
And her skin was oh so soft.
She broke down my resistance,
And now everything is lost.

***She rocks on, rocks on. Just a few more hours till the breaking of the dawn.
She rocks on, rocks on. When the morning sun awakens you,
you'll arise to find her gone.
She's rocked on.***

You don't know what love is for.
You just pretend to give love more.
You lay my love out on the floor.
And I feel like your dirty whore.
Girl, it's time to get down.
One day you'll look for love,
and love won't be found.
Your heart trampled to the ground.

***She rocks on, rocks on. Just a few more hours till the breaking of the dawn.
She rocks on, rocks on. When the morning sun awakens you,
you'll arise to find her gone.
She's rocked on.***

DAISY TURNER

Dear Madam, I am a soldier, and
my speech is rough and plain.
I'm not much used to writing,
and I hate to cause you pain.

But I promised I would do it,
and he thought it might be so.
If it came from one who loved him,
perhaps it would ease the blow.

By now you must have surely
guessed
the truth our pain would hide.
And you'll pardon me for rough
soldier words while I tell you how
he died.

It was in the morass battle, sash rain,
the shot, the shell.
I was standing close beside him,
And I saw him when he fell.
So, I took him in my arms and
laid him on the grass.
It was going against the orders,
but the thought to let it pass.

T'was a mini ball that struck
him; it entered at his side.
But we didn't think it fatal
Till this morning when he died.

"Last night I wanted so to live,
I seemed so young to go.
Last week I passed my birthday,
I was just nineteen, you know.

"When I thought of all I'd planned
to do, it seems so hard to die.
But now I pray to God for grace,
and all my cares gone by."

And here his words grew weaker,
As he partly raised his head.
And whispered, "Goodbye, my love,"
and your soldier boy was dead.

I carved him out a headstone,
as skillful as I could.
And if you wish to find it,
I can tell you where it stood.

I send you back the hymn book,
the cap he used to wear.
the lock I cut the night before
of his bright, curly hair.

I send you back his Bible.
The night before he died,
I turned its leaves together
and read it by his side.

I'll keep the belt he was wearing,
as he told me so to do.
It had a hole upon the side
right where the ball went through.
So now I've done his bidding,
I've nothing more to tell.
But I shall always mourn with
you the boy we loved so well.

THE GUNSLINGER

His face was lined and windblown,
cold can of beans.
He sold his gun for gold and
silver; he sold his gun for a dream.

To die in a blaze of glory,
to a faster gun well known.
To become the fastest gun,
alive, for this he left his home.

Killing for him came easily,
but it wasn't always that way.
He was a farmer who lost it all
and crossed the line one day.

He rode into town to save the farm,
but the bank wouldn't give him a loan.
So, he robbed the bank and gave
the teller the deed to his home.
He wandered for many sleepless nights,
hunted men and sold his gun.
That's how he stayed alive.
Somewhere along the dusty
trail,
the truth in him got lost.
His hatred conquered all he was;
he never knew the cost.

A transformation had taken place;
A killer had been made.
A conscious seared, a heart of stone
to help him ply his trade.

One day he stood upon the dusty
street, two guns to face alone.
His palms were cold and sweaty;
his thoughts referred him home.

As vengeful bullets tore through his flesh,
one in the stomach and two in the chest,
his legs crumpled beneath him, trying to catch his breath.
One final shootout.
It's his turn to rest.

FACES

Their faces and places,
I don't want to see.
There are places and faces
where I don't want to be.

I see the faces.
Turn on my reality.
Can't you see,
I'll never be free
until I face the faces,
that are facing me?

The faces come at night.
Night's the time I dread.
The tear under the sheets.
In fear I pissed my bed.
They always ruled the night
and sometimes ruled the day.
You always thought so badly,
and they told you what to say.

Their faces and places,
I don't want to see.
There are places and faces
where I don't want to be.

I see the faces.
Turn on my reality.
Can't you see
I'll never be free
until I face the faces
that are facing me?

There was this perfect girl,
born from my dreams.
Her vision was so lovely,
but love was not the theme.

Faces destroyed the best of her,
left her soul in empty places.
When I went to ask her why,
she said couldn't you see the faces.

Their faces and places,
I don't want to see.
There are places and faces
where I don't want to be.

I see the faces.
Turn on my reality.
Can't you see
I'll never be free
until I face the faces
that are facing me?

We all have faces
from the present, from the past.
Some are etched in stone,
and some just wouldn't last.
They would try to keep you down,
to keep you in your place.
It's time to give it back
and get up in their face.

Their faces and places,
I don't want to see.
There are places and faces
where I don't want to be.

I see the faces.
Turn on my reality.
Can't you see
I'll never be free
until I face the faces
that are facing me?

JESUS

All I know is that I love him because he died for me.
All I know is that he shed his blood that day on Calvary.
All I know is that he sacrificed, so all the world could live.
Yes, what a price to pay for love;
that's what my Jesus did.

All I know is that they scourged **him** before they hung him on a tree.
All I know is that a crown of thorns, he wore to set me free.
All I know is that he paid the price, my sins he would forgive.
Yes, what a price to pay for love;
that's what my Jesus did.

All I know is that I love him; he was nailed instead of me.
He died upon that rugged cross for all the world to see.
All I know is that he sacrificed, and through him I might live.
Yes, what a price to pay for love.
Well, that's what my Jesus did.

When I Rest

Lord,
If it's time to take me, I have but one request.
That when I lay dying, I'm at my very best.

If it's time for me to die, please help me to be brave.
So, the people who are watching,
by my example might be saved.

Lord,
you know I'd love to see
my two sons grow into men.
I still have lots to offer;
I don't want this life to end.

My little girl,
she needs me.
My place is at her mother's side.
I want to stay and guide them,
but by your will I must abide.

I place them in your keeping.
You always know what's best.
I pray that you preserve them
for your glory
when I rest.

ALMOST HOME

There is so much pain inside of me,
mostly old and yet some new.
The war that rages within my mind,
I'm human. What can I do?

Please forgive me for my foolish
thoughts, for even letting them in.
Thank you, Lord, for forgiving me for the ones I turned to sin.

The freedom that surrounds me,
thick walls within my mind.
I see the glory all around me,
Yet in some hallways, I am blind.

So thank you, God in heaven,
for loving and watching over me.
But especially thanks to Jesus. At last my soul is free.

//

ABOUT THE AUTHOR

Randy McNeil grew up in East Vancouver, with his 4 brothers and his mother. Eventually becoming part of a street gang called the Renfrew Parker Boys. At the age of 24 he gave his life to Christ, he then went on to serve as a prison minister, counseling inmates in various facilities throughout the Lower Mainland area of British Columbia, and later became a pastor of a small church in Sydney, Nova Scotia with his three children and his wife. He passed away in February 2008 at just 51 years of age. In Langley, BC.

This book was published by his daughter as fulfillment of his last request.

CPSIA information can be obtained
at www.ICGtesting.com
Printed in the USA
BVHW010511250322
632416BV00003B/27

9 781039 117211